JUNIOR
BIOGRAPHY
FROM
ANCIENT
CIVILIZATIONS

JULIUS
CAESAR

JOANNE MATTERN

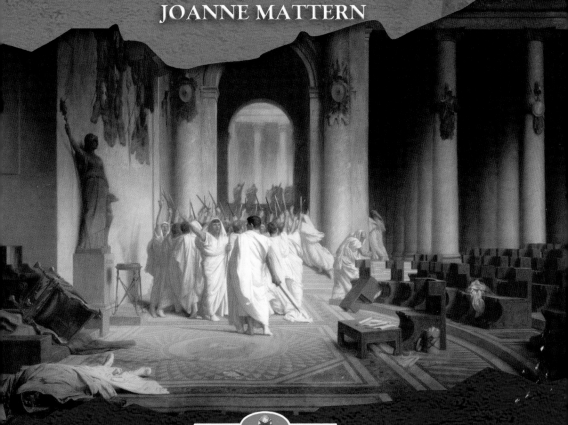

Mitchell Lane
PUBLISHERS

2001 SW 31st Avenue
Hallandale, FL 33009
www.mitchelllane.com

JUNIOR BIOGRAPHY FROM ANCIENT CIVILIZATIONS

Alexander the Great • Archimedes • Augustus Caesar
Buddha • Charlemagne • Cleopatra • Confucius
Genghis Khan • Hammurabi • Hippocrates • Homer
Julius Caesar • King Arthur • Leif Erikson • Marco Polo
Moses • Nero • Plato • Pythagoras • Socrates

Copyright © 2018 by Mitchell Lane Publishers

Printing 1 2 3 4 5 6 7 8 9

ABOUT THE AUTHOR: Joanne Mattern is the author of many books for children on a variety of subjects, including history and biography. She has written many biographies for Mitchell Lane. Joanne loves to learn about people, places, and events and bring historical figures to life for today's readers. She lives in New York with her husband, children, and several pets.

PUBLISHER'S NOTE: The facts on which the story in this book is based have been thoroughly researched. Documentation of such research can be found on pages 44–45. While every possible effort has been made to ensure accuracy, the publisher will not assume liability for damages caused by inaccuracies in the data, and makes no warranty on the accuracy of the information contained herein.

To reflect current usage, we have chosen to use the secular era designations BCE ("before the common era") and CE ("of the common era") instead of the traditional designations BC ("before Christ") and AD (*anno Domini,* "in the year of the Lord").

Library of Congress Cataloging-in-Publication Data

Names: Mattern, Joanne, 1963– author.
Title: Julius Caesar / by Joanne Mattern.
Description: Hallandale, FL : Mitchell Lane Publishers, 2018. | Series: Junior biography from ancient civilizations | Includes bibliographical references and index. | Audience: Grades 4-6. | Audience: Ages 8-11.
Identifiers: LCCN 2017009119 | ISBN 9781680200249 (library bound)
Subjects: LCSH: Caesar, Julius—Juvenile literature. | Heads of state—Rome—Biography—Juvenile literature. | Generals—Rome—Biography—Juvenile literature. | Rome—History—Republic, 265–30 B.C.—Juvenile literature.
Classification: LCC DG261 .M345 2018 | DDC 937/.05092 [B] —dc23
LC record available at https://lccn.loc.gov/2017009119

eBook ISBN: 978-1-618020-025-6

CONTENTS

Chapter One
  Captured by Pirates! 5
  Romulus and Remus and
      the Rise of Rome...............................9
Chapter Two
  Growing Up Roman...............................11
  A Roman Home.....................................13
Chapter Three
  Enemies and Exile.................................15
  The Roman Army...................................19
Chapter Four
  A Great General....................................21
  Slaves and Gladiators 25
Chapter Five
  A Bloody End..27
  A New Calendar....................................39
Chronology 40
Timeline..41
Chapter Notes 42
Further Reading 44
  Books 44
  On the Internet......................................44
  Works Consulted...................................44
Phonetic Pronunciations 46
Glossary..47
Index 48

Phonetic pronunciations of words in **bold**
can be found on page 46.

This portrait of Julius Caesar shows him wearing a wreath of laurel leaves. Wreaths were a sign of honor and respect.

CHAPTER 1
Captured by Pirates!

Julius Caesar* was always eager to learn. As a youth, he had studied with some of the finest scholars of the classical world. Now, in the year 75 BCE, twenty-four-year-old Caesar was on his way across the Aegean Sea to the Greek island of Rhodes to study with the famous Greek philosopher **Apollonius Molon**. However, his thirst for knowledge was about to take a dramatic turn.

Caesar's galley made its way across the turquoise Aegean Sea. The water was clear, dolphins breached the waves to gawk at the ship, and scores of islands rose from the sea. But all was not peaceful. The eastern Mediterranean was home to pirates, and Caesar knew that he might not reach Rhodes without some adventure.

While Rome had a powerful navy, the republic's rulers did not send their ships to crush the brigands. They had a selfish reason for this. Rome needed slaves to work on its plantations and serve its wealthy senators. The pirates gladly sold their captives to Rome. Thus Rome got the slaves it needed, and the pirates got the money they wanted. It was a convenient system—except for those enslaved!

Sure enough, Caesar's ship was attacked as it sailed eastward. The pirates quickly seized the vessel and took Caesar and the other passengers prisoner. They took their captives to their base on the tiny island of **Pharmacusa**, today called **Farmakonisi**. There the pirates told Caesar that they would hold him hostage until he could raise a ransom of twenty gold talents. This was a large sum—about $600,000 in today's money[1], but Caesar was not worried. In fact, he laughed at the pirates!

Caesar scolded them for not knowing who he was. He said that he was worth far more than twenty talents, and demanded that they ask for fifty. The pirates were surprised, but happily agreed to demand the larger figure. Some of Caesar's fellow passengers were released so they could raise the ransom money. Meanwhile, Caesar, a servant, and two friends remained as the pirates' prisoners. However, their captivity didn't go as the pirates had planned.

Though the pirates were bloodthirsty, Caesar was fearless. He did not regard the pirates as his captors. Instead, he treated them like his servants! He bossed them around, and made them listen to speeches. The famous writer **Plutarch** explained, "He held them in such disdain that whenever he lay down to sleep he would . . . order them to stop talking. For eight and thirty days, as if the men were not his watchers, but his royal body-guard, he shared in their sports and exercises with great unconcern. He also wrote poems and sundry speeches which he read aloud to them, and those who did not admire these he would call to their faces illiterate barbarians."[2]

The pirates found Caesar very funny. They admired his pluck, and let him do whatever he wished during the thirty-eight days of his captivity. They didn't even object when Caesar warned them that after he was released, he would return and kill all of them. They thought he was kidding.

After a little more than a month, Caesar's friends delivered the ransom of fifty talents, and the pirates released their captives. Caesar set about getting his revenge. Assembling a small fleet and dozens of armed men, he sailed back to Pharmacusa. The pirates were still there. Perhaps at first they were glad to see their former captive, but Caesar was no longer their friend. He took all the pirates captive and delivered them to a prison in **Pergamon**, today the city of Bergama in Turkey. Caesar reclaimed his fifty talents, as well as all of the pirates' other treasure.

Pergamon was an important city near the Aegean Sea. Today, visitors can see ruins of the ancient city's public buildings.

With the pirates safely in jail, Caesar paid a visit to **Marcus Junius Silanus**, the governor of the Roman province of Asia, today in western Turkey. Caesar demanded that the governor execute the pirates. Junius, however, wanted to sell them as slaves and keep all the money. Stalling, he told Caesar he had not yet decided what to do.

Impatient, Caesar returned to Pergamon and let the pirates out of prison. Then as Plutarch described, he executed them himself, "just as he had often warned them on the island that he would do, when they thought he was joking."[3]

Julius Caesar had a lot of nerve, and he was not afraid to take action. The pirates were not the only people to find that out! Caesar became a Roman politician and general who let nothing stand in his way. He became one of the most powerful people who ever lived, and changed the face of history. However, Caesar became too ambitious. His desire for power led him to a bloody downfall at the hands of his enemies.

This statue of Julius Caesar was made by French sculptor Nicolas Coustou and can be seen at the famous Louvre Museum in Paris, France.

Romulus and Remus and the Rise of Rome

At the time of Caesar's capture by the pirates, Rome was the dominant civilization in the Mediterranean Sea region. According to legend, it was founded by the twin brothers **Romulus** and **Remus**. Their mother was named **Rhea Silva**. She was the daughter of King **Numitor**, who ruled a small city near the future site of Rome. Numitor's brother **Amulius** overthrew him and seized power. When Rhea Silva gave birth to the twins, Amulius ordered a servant to drown them in the **Tiber River**. Otherwise they could threaten his position as king when they grew up. But the servant took pity on the helpless infants. He put them in a basket that carried them downstream.

The basket became entangled in the roots of a tree growing along the river's bank, where a she-wolf discovered the boys. She suckled them until a shepherd named **Faustulus** found them. He and his wife raised them to young manhood. They became the leaders of a group that killed Amulius and restored their grandfather Numitor to power.

Romulus & Remus being suckled by the she-wolf.

Then they founded a city on the site where their basket had drifted ashore. After a quarrel, Romulus killed Remus and named the city after himself. According to the ancient historian **Livy**, this occurred on April 21, 753 BCE. Romulus continued making Rome even larger and more important. Finally he disappeared during a storm. By then the city was on a firm foundation.

Mythology aside, Rome was established sometime in the mid-eighth century BCE. It became a republic in 509 and began gobbling up its close neighbors. By the middle of the second century Rome, controlled much of the Mediterranean shoreline. Caesar would eventually push its borders even further.

This portrait of Julius Caesar was painted in 1892 by German artist Clara Grosch and shows him as an older man.

CHAPTER 2
Growing Up Roman

Born around 100 BCE, Caesar's full name was **Gaius** Julius Caesar. He had two older sisters, although only one, named Julia, would live to adulthood. Caesar's father was a government official called a *praetor*, or judge. His mother, Aurelia Cotta, took care of the home and her family. Caesar was descended from the Julii, one of Rome's most ancient and powerful families. They claimed to be the offspring of Venus, the goddess of love.

When Caesar was born, Rome was perhaps the largest city in the world. It was the capital of a republic that stretched from today's France to North Africa and Turkey. Hundreds of thousands of people lived in the capital city itself. Some, like Caesar's family, were from the nobility and upper class. Others were ordinary citizens. The majority were servants or slaves. Caesar's family was important and lived well, but they were not wealthy. Like most families of that class, they lived in a large detached house called a villa, and had several servants.

When Caesar was a little boy, he probably spent much of his time playing. Roman children's favorite toys included balls and dolls. They also played with carved wooden animals, marbles made out of glass, and a board game similar to checkers called *latrunculi,* or the game of brigands. Boys enjoyed wrestling and playing soldier with child-sized wooden swords and helmets. In another popular game, players on one team tried to drag their opponents across a line drawn on the ground.

When Caesar was six or seven years old, he started school. At that time, wealthy Roman boys attended small schools with a single teacher. At first they studied simple math, and how to read and write in Latin. Students memorized and recited long literary passages, and lists of laws. Some girls went to school, but they usually left after a few years. In Roman times, girls were destined to become wives and mothers, so they needed to learn how to run a household.

When most boys were about eleven, they graduated to secondary school. There they studied history, geography, astronomy, math, grammar, and music. They learned Greek as well as Latin, studied the history of Greece and Rome, and read books by classical Greek and Roman authors.

Because Caesar came from a noble family, he had a private teacher, or tutor. Caesar's first teacher was a Greek scholar named **Marcus Antonius Gnipho**, who was highly respected in both Greece and Rome. He quickly realized that Caesar was very smart. Gnipho taught his prize student many things, including training him to be a skilled orator. Oratory, or public speaking, was considered a key skill, and anyone who wanted to be a politician learned to speak well in public. Gnipho also taught Caesar to write poetry and plays.

Above all, Gnipho taught Caesar to appreciate Greek language and culture. While Rome was powerful, it was strongly influenced by the older Greek civilization.

Caesar probably studied with Gnipho until he was fifteen years old. Then an event happened that changed his world.

A Roman Home

Romans lived in great luxury. Their villas were large and beautifully decorated structures built of stone or brick, with a roof of red clay tiles. Each room opened onto a central courtyard, called an *atrium*, that provided light and fresh air. A walled garden was located at the rear of the house.

Romans filled their homes with beautiful furniture. The rich slept on cushioned beds and couches decorated with gems. Wealthy Romans banqueted lying on couches grouped in three, called a *triclinium*. Colorful frescoes covered the walls while mosaics were laid out on the floors. Painted marble statues decorated the rooms.

Rich Roman enjoyed central heating, running water, and toilets in their homes. Villas were heated by a furnace called a *hypocaust,* which forced hot air underneath the floor.

Poor Romans lived a much simpler lifestyle. Most lived in *insulae*, or apartment buildings grouped around a central courtyard. Some insulae were solidly built of stone or brick. Others were poorly built of mud bricks or wood. These insulae were overcrowded and did not have running water or toilets. They often collapsed. It was not unusual for fires to spread through insulae, burning the buildings to the ground.

Remains of the top floors of an insula near the Capitolium and the Aracoeli in Rome

A statue of Julius Caesar in front of the Parliament building in Vienna, Austria.

CHAPTER 3
Enemies and Exile

In 85 BCE when Caesar was about fifteen years old, his father Gaius Julius Caesar the Elder died on a business trip. This made Caesar the head of his family, responsible for taking care of his mother and sister.

Caesar was now old enough to marry. As was the custom in classical Rome, his father had chosen a bride when his son was just a little boy. Her name was **Cossutia**. However, when Caesar's father died, the teenager decided not to go through with the wedding. Instead, he married a woman named **Cornelia** in 84 BCE. Her father, **Cinna**, was one of the most powerful men in Rome. Their daughter, Julia, was born a year later.

Because Caesar was from a noble family, he was expected to have a career in the government. The idea appealed to him. After the wedding, Caesar became an officer in the Roman army. He also began working for the government. Caesar was popular, well-spoken, and good-looking. He seemed to be on the path to a golden future.

While Caesar was growing up, Rome was a republic. The city and state were controlled by six hundred citizens called the Senate. Each senator came from an important family. The Senate elected two senior officials every year, called consuls. Their responsibility was to ensure the Senate and the army ran smoothly. Consuls had enormous power, and often rewarded their followers with good jobs.

All men born in Rome were citizens, unless they were slaves. Women could also be citizens, though they didn't have as many rights as men. Citizens had more rights and privileges than noncitizens. One of the most important privileges was the right to vote. Citizens were also exempt from paying some taxes.

The Curia Julia was the third Curia, or Senate House, in ancient Rome. Julius Caesar built the Curia Julia in 44 BCE to replace the older Curia built by Sulla.

In addition to citizens and noncitizens, Rome was divided between rich and poor. Rich people were called patricians. They owned estates, and came from noble families. All other citizens were called plebians. Even though some plebians were rich, they were not considered as good as the patricians.

As Caesar was growing up, two different groups in Rome were fighting each other. One faction, called the *Populares*, wanted to give more power to the common people. The other group, the *Optimates*, wanted the senators to remain in control. Caesar and his family were linked with the Populares. His father-in-law, Cinna, was also one of the leaders of the Populares.

Inside the Curia Julia, the restored Senate House

The exterior of the Curia Julia

The rivalry between the Populares and the Optimates often turned violent. In 82 BCE, Cinna was murdered. The leader of the Optimates, a man called **Sulla**, arrived in Rome with an army. The Senate quickly named him Rome's dictator. That meant he was the only leader.

Sulla asked to see Caesar. He knew Caesar was from a powerful family and had a promising future. Sulla wanted Caesar on his side. He told Caesar that he should break his ties with the Populares. He even advised Caesar to divorce his wife Cornelia, since she was Cinna's daughter. If Caesar did these things, Sulla said, Caesar would show he was loyal to Rome and could continue his political career.

Caesar rejected Sulla's suggestions. He refused to divorce his wife and change his opinion. He did not want any part of Sulla's plans.

Sulla was angered by Caesar's choice. Caesar and his friends knew that Sulla was now his mortal enemy. To save his life, Caesar fled Rome and went into hiding in the hills outside the city.

After several months, Sulla pardoned Caesar. However, the young man was not keen to return to Rome. Instead, he took the opportunity to gain experience that would help his political career. Caesar had many important friends, and they were able to get him a job working for **Marcus Minucius Thermus**, who was the Roman military governor of the province of Asia.

Working for Thermus was an excellent opportunity for Caesar. He learned about the world outside of Rome. He also gained military experience. One of the highlights of his time in Asia occurred in 80 BCE, when he took part in the siege of the city of **Mytilene** on the Aegean island of Lesbos. Caesar was awarded a military honor called the corona civica, or civic crown, because of his important work during the battle.

Caesar's old enemy Sulla died in 78 BCE. It was finally safe for him to return to Rome. By this time, Caesar was known as a skilled orator and a seasoned warrior. His star would continue to rise.

The Roman Army

For many years, landowners who could afford to own their weapons formed most of the Roman army. But many wars wore down their numbers. In 107 BCE, the consul Marius reformed the army. He opened it to all Romans. For men without much money, it was ideal. Rome itself equipped them. The army became professional and soldiers could count on being paid steadily. Many soldiers served for at least 20 years before retiring.

Soldiers were divided into legions. Each legion had some 4,200-4,800 fighters, divided into ten smaller groups called cohorts.[1] Each legionnaire was equipped with armor and weapons like a sword or spear.

Roman soldiers followed strict discipline. Falling asleep on guard duty was punishable by death. A Roman soldier would never dream of deserting his post, even if he faced superior forces and knew he would likely be killed. Desertion was considered so shameful that a soldier would never be accepted by his family and would have to leave home forever.

Modern-day men dress up as Roman soldiers to re-enact a battle.

Caesar was a powerful military leader. This painting shows him inspecting his troops.

CHAPTER 4
A Great General

In 75 BCE, Caesar tracked down the pirates of Pharmacusa, as he had vowed he would. He was already well-known in the capital, but slaying the pirates made people admire him even more.

By 73 BCE, Caesar, now twenty-seven years old, was ready to take on even more responsibility. He was not only admired, but also his patrician family background gave him many important connections. Caesar used those contacts to rise to positions that gave him more experience and power.

One of the positions Caesar held was priest of Jupiter. The ancient Romans believed in many gods and goddesses. Each had his or her own special role. For example, Venus was the goddess of love, Mars the god of war, and Apollo the sun deity. The king and queen of the gods were Jupiter and Juno. The Romans believed their deities protected Rome and influenced everyday life. To honor their gods, they built them temples and celebrated their feast days. Priests, who were chosen from Roman leaders, offered up prayers and sacrifices. As priest of Jupiter, Caesar played an important role in Roman life.

In 69 BCE, Caesar was sent to the Roman province of Spain for a year. Just before he left, his wife Cornelia died. After he returned from Spain, Caesar married a woman named **Pompeia**. Like his first wife, Pompeia came from a powerful family. Her cousin was a famous general named **Pompey**. Her grandfather was Caesar's old enemy, Sulla. Pompeia was also very rich. Her money helped Caesar gain even more power.

By 65 BCE, Caesar was put in charge of maintaining all of Rome's public buildings, as well as organizing all public entertainment. Caesar made the most of his new job. He had become friends with a powerful and rich senator named **Marcus Licinius Crassus**. Caesar used Crassus's fortune and Pompeia's money to pay for huge public festivals. He organized gladiator battles and religious festivals. The people loved the excitement, and Caesar became even more popular.

Two years later in 63 BCE, Caesar was appointed Rome's chief priest. Though he was personally not particularly religious, being high priest was another powerful position that allowed him to develop even more connections. The following year, Caesar was elected praetor, or senior judge. That year, he also divorced his wife. Later he married **Calpurnia**, who was the daughter of a rich senator. At the same time, Caesar's daughter, Julia, married the successful general Pompey.

In 61 BCE, Caesar was sent back to Spain to act as the province's governor. When he returned to Rome a year later, he applied for the position of senior consul. Supported by his friends Pompey and Crassus, Caesar won the prestigious job. The three men became so powerful that they were called the Triumvirate.

A consul only served for one year. After his term was over, Caesar became governor of three different provinces, **Cisalpine Gaul**, **Transalpine Gaul** and **Illyricum**. Today these areas are northern Italy, southern France, and Croatia. Caesar soon faced trouble. Across the Alps north of Rome was Gaul, the rich homeland of the Gallic tribes. Over the next seven years, Caesar and his powerful army battled and defeated some 300 different tribes. His army faced millions of warriors.[1]

Caesar was also very interested in the Gauls' culture. During his time there, he took notes about the tribes' customs, religion, and daily

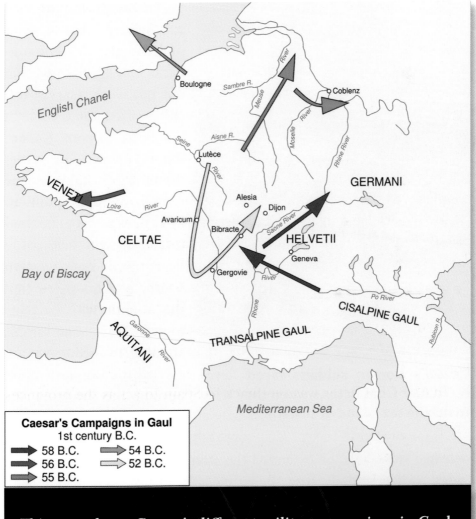

Caesar's Campaigns in Gaul
1st century B.C.
- 58 B.C.
- 56 B.C.
- 55 B.C.
- 54 B.C.
- 52 B.C.

This map shows Caesar's different military campaigns in Gaul during the first century BCE.

lives. His book about them, *The Gallic Wars*, remains an important historical source.

Caesar was always eager to expand Rome's territory. In 55 BCE and again in 54, he sent ships and troops from the European continent to the island of Britain. But the tribes living in Britain fought back so fiercely that Caesar pulled his legionnaires back. Though his invasion did not work, Caesar was still praised for trying. In his book *Life of Caesar*, Plutarch wrote, "His expedition into Britain was the most famous testimony of his courage. For he was the first who brought a fleet into the western ocean, or who sailed into the Atlantic with an army to make war . . . and in his attempt to occupy it he carried the Roman empire beyond the limits of the known world."[2]

Caesar's Roman soldiers faced fierce resistance from natives when they tried to invade the island of Britain.

When Caesar finally defeated the Gauls, he extended the Roman Republic across what is today Switzerland, Austria, Belgium, and France. When people in Rome heard the news, they praised Caesar as a military genius. However, not everyone in Rome was happy. Caesar's power and his loyal army made some Romans very nervous.

Slaves and Gladiators

Like many pre-modern civilizations, ancient Rome depended on the labor of slaves. Some were captured by pirates or became prisoners during wartime. Children who had no families often became slaves. The law even permitted fathers to sell their children into slavery if they needed money.

All wealthy Romans had slaves. They would buy them in the market, just as they might buy new clothes or food. Slaves with a particular skill such as cooking, or who were young and strong, cost more money.

Slaves did all kinds of labor. Some worked on plantations. Some toiled in workshops or mines. Others worked in homes, cooking, cleaning, and taking care of children. Slaves even dressed their masters and carried them around on fancy seats called litters. A slave could only win his freedom if his master gave it to him, or if he somehow managed to raise enough money to buy his way out of slavery.

No one knows exactly how many slaves lived in ancient Rome, but historians believe slaves made up about a quarter of the population.[3] A rich man might own as many as 500 slaves. When Rome became an empire, some emperors had more than 20,000![4]

Gladiators were another type of slave, though some were prisoners of war or convicted criminals. They fought, often to the death, at public games which were one of the most popular forms of entertainment in Roman life. Sent to training schools where they learned how to fight and use weapons, some gladiators fought with swords and shields. Others fought on horseback or chariots.

Not everyone was a fan of gladiator spectacles. The famous philosopher **Seneca** described a match this way: "The men have no defensive armor. They are exposed to blows at all points, and no one ever strikes in vain. . . . There is no helmet or shield to deflect the weapon. What is the need of defensive armor, or of skill? All these mean delaying death. . . . The spectators demand that the slayer shall face the man who is to slay him in his turn; and they always reserve the latest conqueror for another butchering. The outcome of every fight is death, and the means are fire and sword."[5]

Cicero was probably wrong. While the lives of gladiators were usually brutal and short, most fights apparently didn't result in death. The majority ended when one of the combatants was seriously injured. In some cases, fights would drag on and the spectators would become bored. In others, the fight would match evenly skilled gladiators and be especially exciting. In such cases, both fighters left the arena relatively **unscathed**.[6]

A statue of Julius Caesar in the Vatican Museum in Rome.

CHAPTER 5
A Bloody End

While Caesar was campaigning in Gaul, things were not going well in Rome. A power struggle was raging between the old ruling families and the new Triumvirate. Some of the senators spread rumors that Caesar had become too powerful. They hinted that he might even be more powerful than the great general Pompey. This idea angered Pompey greatly.

In 53 BCE, Crassus, who was the third member of the Triumvirate, was killed in battle fighting the Parthians, an ancient civilization based in today's Iran. After his death, the situation became even more violent. Pompey was elected consul. He ordered Caesar to return to Rome from Cisalpine Gaul to face charges of treason. Caesar complied, but he did not go back to Rome alone. He brought his loyal legionnaires with him.

In 49 BCE Caesar and one of his legions crossed the Rubicon River north of Rome. Under Roman law, generals were not allowed to cross the waterway with their troops. Crossing the shallow river marked a point of no return, and set off a civil war.

This painting shows Julius Caesar (in red) accepting the surrender of Vercingetorix, the leader of the Gauls, after winning the Battle of Alesia in 52 BCE. Caesar often showed little mercy to captured enemies. He dragged Vercingetorix to Rome in chains and executed him six years later.

This illustration shows Caesar and his army crossing the Rubicon.
Caesar's action was one of the boldest and most daring acts of his life.

When Pompey and the other senators heard that Caesar was heading toward Rome with his army, they fled to Greece. Caesar followed them and in 48 BCE, defeated Pompey at the Battle of **Pharsalus**. Pompey escaped across the Mediterranean Sea to Egypt, and Caesar chased after him. There he got a surprise. The fourteen-year-old king of Egypt, **Ptolemy** XIII, had Pompey murdered. He presented Pompey's head to Caesar as a gift. Caesar had won the civil war. He was now the most powerful man in the Roman Republic.

Caesar stayed in Egypt for a year. In 45 BCE, he defeated the last of Pompey's followers at the Battle of Munda in today's Spain. Finally he returned to Rome in triumph where he held not one but four victory parades. His soldiers carried placards reading, "Veni, Vidi, Vici," which is Latin for "I came, I saw, I conquered." Caesar had made the

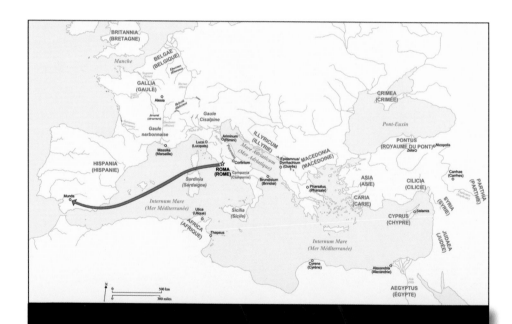

This map shows Caesar's campaigns from Rome to Munda in 46–45 BCE.

This is one of nine paintings by Italian artist Andrea Andreani called *The Triumphs of Caesar*. Created between 1484 and 1492, the series celebrates Caesar's military victories in Gaul.

phrase famous in a letter he sent to the Roman Senate in 46 BCE announcing his quick victory in the Battle of Zela in today's Turkey.

The Senate named Caesar dictator, or sole leader of Rome. Caesar did not waste any time making changes. He added new members to the Senate, including men who had fought in his army. He added more officials to help run the state. Most of all, Caesar took power away from the patricians and gave more power to the plebians.

By 44 BCE, it seemed that no one could stop Caesar. However, the noble families were unhappy with his power and the changes he was making. In March, Caesar called a meeting of the Senate and demanded that he be made emperor, officially ending the republic. That was the last straw for the noble families. They began plotting against Caesar, and agreed they would have to kill him.

Sixty conspirators planned Caesar's assassination. They were led by two of Pompey's former soldiers, **Brutus** and **Cassius**. Caesar had pardoned both men after the war, and considered them his friends. Brutus and Cassius determined the best place to murder Caesar would be in the Senate. They arranged to meet him there on March 15. That day is known as the Ides of March.

When Caesar entered the Senate, a group of senators surrounded him. Caesar wasn't surprised. He thought they wished to question him about his request to be anointed emperor. Instead, one of the men pulled out a dagger and stabbed Caesar. The others did the same. Caesar collapsed dead on the floor with twenty-three stab wounds.

The people of Rome were horrified when they heard that Caesar had been murdered. People ran through the streets, rioting and destroying property. Caesar's funeral was held in the Forum, which was Rome's central square. Thousands attended.

Caesar had named his adopted great-nephew, **Octavian**, to assume power after he died. Octavian was the grandson of Caesar's sister, Julia. Most of Rome's citizens supported Octavian, and so did the army. However, many members of the Senate did not. A second civil war broke out. In 42 BCE, the Senate was defeated. Another civil war

A statue of Augustus Caesar in the Vatican Museum in Rome. The small figure by his right leg is Cupid riding a dolphin. It indicates his mythical connection to the goddess Venus (Cupid's mother), since Julius Caesar (his adopted father), claimed descent from Venus.

These ruins are all that remain of the Forum of Julius Caesar and the Temple of Venus Genetrix in Rome. The Temple was dedicated to Venus Genetrix, the goddess of motherhood, by Caesar in 46 BCE.

followed, but by 27 BCE, Octavian had won control. He eventually became the first Roman emperor and changed his name to **Augustus Caesar.** That marked the end of the Roman Republic.

Julius Caesar expanded Rome's possessions into one of the world's greatest realms. At its height three centuries later, the Roman Empire had expanded to include an estimated sixty-five million people, or one in five people on Earth.[1] The Roman Empire that Caesar helped create would be the most powerful in the world for more than four hundred years and is still considered one of the world's greatest civilizations.

Because Caesar was so important, people have been writing about him for many centuries. His own works tell part of the story, and so do other writings from ancient Rome. Other information comes from statues and coins that bear his image. Even though he lived more than two thousand years ago, Caesar is still known as one of the most important figures in history.

A New Calendar

Julius Caesar introduced the solar calendar we use today. For centuries, scientists had tried to create a calendar that remained in sync with the changing seasons. This had proven difficult because of the length of time it takes the Earth to move around the sun. Since the old Roman calendar had 355 days, periodically extra days or months had to be added. In 45 BCE, after consulting with astronomers and mathematicians, Caesar created the Julian calendar based on a 365.25-day annual cycle with eleven months of 30 or 31 days and February with 28. Every fourth year a leap day was added to February. In his honor, the month of Quintilis was named Iulius or July.

However, since the Earth actually takes 365.2425 days to rotate around the sun, Caesar's new calendar still lost time over the centuries. To fix this problem, in 1582 Pope Gregory XIII ordered a calendar reform. Thirteen days were added in the Gregorian calendar to realign it with the seasons.

Months (Roman)	Lengths before 45 BC	Lengths as of 45 BC	Months (English)
Ianuarius	29	31	January
Februarius	28 (in common years) In intercalary years: 23 if Intercalaris is variable 23/24 if Intercalaris is fixed	28 (leap years: 29)	February
Mercedonius/ Intercalaris	0 (leap years: variable (27/28 days) or fixed)	(abolished)	—
Martius	31	31	March
Aprilis	29	30	April
Maius	31	31	May
Iunius	29	30	June
Quintilis (Iulius)	31	31	July
Sextilis (Augustus)	29	31	August
September	29	30	September
October	31	31	October
November	29	30	November
December	29	31	December

BCE

ca. 100	Gaius Julius Caesar is born in Rome.
ca. 97	One of Caesar's two older sisters dies.
ca. 94	Caesar starts school.
ca. 89	Caesar's father arranges a marriage between Caesar and Cossutia.
ca. 85	Caesar's father dies and he officially becomes an adult.
ca. 84	Caesar marries Cornelia.
ca. 83	Caesar's daughter, Julia, is born.
81	Sulla tries to make Caesar divorce his wife; Caesar refuses and leaves Rome.
80	Caesar joins the staff of Marcus Minucius Thermus in the province of Asia; he wins military honors after the battle of Mytilene.
78	Caesar returns to Rome when Sulla dies.
ca. 75	Caesar is captured by pirates. After being freed, he tracks down his captors and kills them.
69	Caesar's wife, Cornelia, dies.
67	Caesar marries Pompeia.
65	Caesar is put in charge of Rome's public entertainment.
62	Caesar divorces Pompeia.
60	Caesar is elected as consul and forms the Triumvirate with Pompey and Crassus.
59	Caesar's daughter, Julia, marries Pompey.
58	Caesar goes to war against Gaul.
55	Caesar leads Rome's first military invasion of Britain.
53	Rome faces public riots and political turmoil.
49	Caesar and his army enter Rome.
48	Caesar defeats Pompey's army at Pharsalus, Greece.
46	Caesar returns to Rome and is named dictator.
44	Caesar asks the Senate to proclaim him emperor; sixty men plot Caesar's assassination and murder him on March 15.

BCE

149–146   Rome and Carthage fight the Third Punic War; Rome defeats Carthage and takes control of land in North Africa.

146   Rome conquers Greece.

ca. 100   Julius Caesar is born.

48   Ptolemy III and his sister, Cleopatra, fight a civil war in Egypt.

45   Rome begins using the Julian calendar.

44   Julius Caesar is assassinated; his nephew Octavian takes power along with two other men.

30   Rome conquers Egypt.

27   Octavian becomes the first Roman emperor and takes the name Augustus Caesar.

ca. 4   Jesus of Nazareth is born.

CE 14   Augustus Caesar dies.

Mausoleum of Augustus Caesar in Rome, Italy

Chapter 1: Captured by Pirates!

1. Daven Hiskey, "When Julius Caesar Was Kidnapped By Pirates, He Demanded They Increase His Ransom," *Mental Floss*, November 19, 2012. http://mentalfloss.com/article/13089/when-julius-caesar-was-kidnapped-pirates-he-demanded-they-increase-his-ransom

2. Plutarch, *The Life of Julius Caesar*. http://penelope.uchicago.edu/Thayer/E/Roman/Texts/Plutarch/Lives/Caesar*.htm

3. Ibid.

4. Christopher Wanjek, *Bad Medicine: Misconceptions and Misuses Revealed* (Hoboken, NJ: John Wiley & Sons, 2003), p. 5.

Chapter 3: Enemies and Exiles

1. Charlotte Bernard, *Caesar and Rome* (New York: Henry Holt and Company, 1996), p. 38.

Chapter 4: A Great General

1. Ellen Galford, *Julius Caesar: The Boy Who Conquered an Empire* (Washington, DC: The National Geographic Society, 2007), p. 43.

2. "Plutarch on Julius Caesar." Excerpted from Plutarch, "Caesar" in *The Lives of Noble Grecians and Romans*, John Dryden and Arthur H. Clough, trans. and ed., vol. 3 (Boston: Little, Brown and Co., 1902), http://www.shsu.edu/~his_ncp/PluCaes.html

3. Plutarch, *The Life of Julius Caesar*.
   http://penelope.uchicago.edu/Thayer/E/Roman/
   Texts/Plutarch/Lives/Caesar*.html
4. Chris Trueman, "Roman Slaves."
   http://www.historylearningsite.co.uk/
   roman_slaves.htm
5. "The Roman Gladiator."
   http://penelope.uchicago.edu/~grout/
   encyclopaedia_romana/gladiators/gladiators.html
6. Evan Andrews, "Ten Things You May Not
   Know About Roman Gladiators." History.com.
   http://www.history.com/news/history-lists/
   10-things-you-may-not-know-about-roman-
   gladiators

Chapter 5: A Bloody End

1. "Roman Empire Population."
   http://www.unrv.com/empire/roman-population.
   php

Books

Hunter, Nick. *Julius Caesar*. Hero Journals. Chicago: Raintree, 2013.

Medina, Nico. *Who Was Julius Caesar?* New York: Grosset & Dunlap, 2014.

Rinaldo, Denise. *Julius Caesar: Dictator for Life*. Wicked History. New York: Franklin Watts, 2009.

On the Internet

"Biography of Julius Caesar." Ducksters.com
http://www.ducksters.com/history/ancient_rome/julius_caesar.php

"Discover Ancient Rome." History for Kids.net
http://www.historyforkids.net/ancient-rome.html

"Julius Caesar Facts." Primary Facts.com
http://primaryfacts.com/1316/julius-caesar-facts/

"The Life of Julius Caesar." Social Studies for Kids.com
http://www.socialstudiesforkids.com/articles/worldhistory/juliuscaesar1.htm

"Ten Facts About Ancient Rome." National Geographic for Kids
http://www.ngkids.co.uk/did-you-know/10-facts-about-the-ancient-Romans

Works Consulted

Andrews, Evan. "Ten Things You May Not Know About Roman Gladiators." History.com. http://www.history.com/news/history-lists/10-things-you-may-not-know-about-roman-gladiators

Bernard, Charlotte. *Caesar and Rome*. New York: Henry Holt and Company, 1996.

Bruns, Roger. *Julius Caesar*. New York: Chelsea House Publishers, 1987.

Galford, Ellen. *Julius Caesar: The Boy Who Conquered an Empire*. Washington, DC: The National Geographic Society, 2007.

Garcia, Brittany. "Romulus and Remus." *Ancient History Encyclopedia*, October 4, 2013. http://www.ancient.eu/Romulus_and_Remus/

"The Gregorian Calendar." Time and Date.com.
http://www.timeanddate.com/calendar/
gregorian-calendar.html

Hiskey, Daven. "When Julius Caesar Was Kidnapped By
Pirates, He Demanded They Increase His Ransom,"
Mental Floss, November 19, 2012. http://mentalfloss.com/
article/13089/when-julius-caesar-was-kidnapped-pirates-he-
demanded-they-increase-his-ransom

"The Julian Calendar." Time and Date.com.
http://www.timeanddate.com/calendar/julian-calendar.html

"Julius Caesar." PBS.org. http://www.pbs.org/empires/romans/
empire/julius-caesar.html

"Julius Caesar—Biography." Biography.com.
http://www.biography.com/people/julius-caesar-
9192504#synopsis

"Julius Caesar: Historical Background." Vroma.org.
http://www.vroma.org/~bmcmanus/caesar.html

Lendering, Jona. "Gaius Julius Caesar —A Biography in
Twelve Parts." Livius.org. http://www.livius.org/caa-can/
caesar/caesar01.html

Plutarch, *The Life of Julius Caesar*. http://penelope.uchicago.
edu/Thayer/E/Roman/Texts/Plutarch/Lives/Caesar*.html

"Plutarch on Julius Caesar." Excerpted from Plutarch, "Caesar"
in *The Lives of Noble Grecians and Romans*, John Dryden
and Arthur H. Clough, tr. and ed., vol. 3 (Boston: Little,
Brown and Co., 1902). http://www.shsu.edu/~his_ncp/
PluCaes.html

"Roman Empire Population." http://www.unrv.com/empire/
roman-population.php

"The Roman Gladiator." http://penelope.uchicago.edu/~grout/
encyclopaedia_romana/gladiators/gladiators.html

"The Romans—Housing." History on the Net.com.
http://www.historyonthenet.com/romans/housing.htm

Trueman, Chris. "Roman Slaves."
http://www.historylearningsite.co.uk/roman_slaves.htm

Wanjek, Christopher. *Bad Medicine: Misconceptions and
Misuses Revealed*. Hoboken, NJ: John Wiley & Sons, 2003.

PHONETIC PRONUNCIATIONS

Amulius (uh-MYOO-lee-us)
Apollonius Molon (ap-uh-LOH-nee-us MOH-lon)
Augustus (uh-GUSS-tuss)
Aurelia Cotta (uh-REEL-yuh KOT-uh)
Brutus (BROO-tuss)
Calpurnia (kal-PUR-nee-uh)
Cassius (CASH-us)
Cinna (SIN-uh)
Cisalpine Gaul (siss-AL-pine GAWL)
Cornelia (kor-NEEL-yuh)
Cossutia (caw-SUE-shuh)
Farmakonisi (far-mah-koh-NEE-see)
Faustulus (FOWS-tyoo-luhs)
Gaius (GAH-yoos)
Illyricum (ih-LEER-ih-kum)
Julius Caesar (JOOL-ee-uhs SEE-zar)
Livy (LIH-vee)
Marcus Antonius Gnipho (MAR-kus an-TONE-ee-us guh-NEE-foh)
Marcus Junius (MAR-kus JOON-ee-us)
Marcus Licinius Crassus (MAR-kus lih-SIN-ee-us KRAS-us)
Marcus Minucius Thermus (MAR-kus min-OO-shee-us THER-mus)
Mytilene (mit-il-EE-nee)
Numitor (NOO-muh-tohr)
Octavian (ok-TAH-vee-an)
Pergamon (PURR-guh-muhn)
Pharmacusa (far-mah-KOO-suh)
Pharsalus (far-SALE-us)
Plutarch (PLOO-tark)
Pompeia (pawm-PEE-uh)
Pompey (PAWM-pee)
Ptolemy (TAH-luh-mee)
Remus (REE-muhss)
Rhea Silva (REE-uh SIL-vuh)
Romulus (RAHM-yoo-luhss)
Seneca (SEN-uh-kuh)
Sulla (SOO-lah)
Tiber River (TYE-buhr RIHV-uhr)
Transalpine Gaul (trans-AL-pine GAWL)

PHOTO CREDITS: Cover, p. 1—Jean-Léon Gérôme/Walters Art Museum/Public domain; p. 4—Timelife Pictures/Getty Images; p. 7—Petitfrere/Dreamstime; p. 8—Carole Raddato/cc-by sa 2.0; p. 9—BruceBlaus/ Blausen.com staff. "Blausen gallery 2014". Wikiversity Journal of Medicine/cc-by sa 3.0; p. 10—Clara Grosch/Public domain; p. 13—Lalupa/Public domain; p. 14—Jozef Sedmak/Dreamstime; pp. 16–17—Baloncici/Dreamstime; p. 17 (inset)—Dneale52/Public domain; p. 19—Maisna/Dreamstime; pp. 20, 33—Library of Congress; p. 23—Sémhur/cc-by sa 3.0; p. 24—Photos.com; p. 26—Ingvar Bjork/Dreamstime; pp. 28–29—Lionel Royer/Museum Crozatier/Public domain; pp. 30–31—Dorling Kindersley/Thinkstock; p. 32—historicair/cc-by sa 3.0; p. 35—Till Niermann/cc-by sa 3.0; pp. 36–37—Scaliger/Dreamstime; p. 38—Vincenzo Camuccini; p. 39—cc-by sa; p. 41—ryarwood/cc-by sa 2.0.

ambitious (am-BISH-us)—having a strong desire to succeed

ancient (AYN-shunt)—very old

assassinate (uh-SASS-uh-nate)—to kill someone who is well-known or important

atrium (AY-tree-uhm)—the central room of a Roman villa, open to the sky at the center and usually having a pool for the collection of rain water

barbarians (bahr-BAIR-ee-uhnz)—a person without culture or education

captivity (kap-TIV-i-tee)—the state or period of being held, imprisoned, enslaved, or confined

citizens (SIT-uh-zenz)—members of a state who owe loyalty to the government and receive certain rights and protection

civil war (SIV-uhl WAR)—a war between different groups in the same country

cohort (KOH-hawrt)—one of the ten divisions in an ancient Roman legion, numbering from 300 to 600 soldiers

consuls (KON-suhlz)—two elected officials who held the highest authority in the Roman Republic

dictator (DIK-tay-tuhr)—a ruler who has either taken or been given complete control of the government

emperor (EM-per-er)—the ruler of an empire

empire (EM-pire)—a large area of land ruled by one person or government

execute (EK-si-kyoot)—to put to death

gladiator (GLAD-ee-ay-tuhr)—someone who is given weapons and forced to fight for public entertainment

hypocaust (HAHY-puh-kawst)—a system of channels in the floor of ancient Roman buildings that provided central heating by distributing the heat from a furnace

insula (IN-suh-luh)—housing for poor Romans

legions (LEE-junz)—units of the Roman army

noble (NO-buhl)—powerful, of high rank

oratory (OR-uh-tor-ee)—the art of public speaking

pardoned (PAR-duhnd)—forgave

patricians (puh-TRISH-uhnz)—members of one of Rome's old land-owning families

philosophers (fuh-LOSS-uh-ferz)—people who study truth and wisdom

plantations (plan-TAY-shunz)—large farms found in warm climates

plebians (PLEE-bee-uhnz)—members of a Roman family that did not have noble blood; commoners

praetor (PREE-ter)—an elected magistrate in the ancient Roman republic

province (PROV-uhnss)—an area within an empire

ransom (RAN-sum)—money demanded by kidnappers

republic (ruh-PUB-lik)—a country governed by officials who are elected or appointed

sacrifices (SAK-ruh-fy-sez)—offerings made to a god

scholars (SKOL-urz)—people who have a great deal of knowledge

Senate (SEN-it)—a group of officials that governed Rome

treason (TREE-zuhn)—the crime of betraying your country

triclinium (try-KLIN-ee-uhn)—a couch extending along three sides of a table, for reclining on at meals

tutor (TOO-tuhr)—a private teacher

unscathed (un-SKATHD)—without being hurt or damaged

Aegean Sea 5
Amulius 9
Apollonius Molon 5
Augustus Caesar 38
Aurelia Cotta 11
Battle of Munda 32
Britain 24
Brutus 34
Calpurnia 22
Cassius 34
Cinna 15, 17, 18
Cisalpine Gaul 22, 27
consuls 16, 27
Cornelia 15, 18, 22
Cossutia 15
deities 21
Faustulus 9
Gaius Julius Caesar the Elder 11,
  15
Gallic Wars, The 24
Gaul 22–24, 27
gladiators 25
Gregorian calendar 39
Ides of March 34
Illyricum 22
Julia (Caesar's daughter) 15, 22
Julia (Caesar's sister) 11, 34
Julian calendar 39
Julius Caesar
  appointed Rome's chief priest
    22
  assassination of 34
  battles Gallic tribes 23–24
  becomes officer in Roman
    army 15
  becomes part of the
    Triumvirate 22
  becomes priest of Jupiter 21
  birth of 11
  captured by pirates 6–8
  childhood of 12
  death of father 15

demands to be named
    emperor 34
  exile of 18
  first marriage of 15
  funeral of 34
  is named dictator 34
  put in charge of public
    entertainment 22
  sends ships to Britain 24
  serves with Marcus Minucius
    Thermus 18
  war with Pompey 27, 32
Life of Caesar 24
Livy 9
Marcus Antonius Gnipho 12
Marcus Junius Silanus 8
Marcus Licinius Crassus 22, 27
Marcus Minucius Thermus 18
Mytilene 18
Numitor 9
Octavian 34, 38
Optimates 17–18
Pergamon 7, 8
Pharmacusa 6, 7, 21
Pharsalus 32
pirates 5–8, 21
Plutarch 6, 8, 24
Pompeia 22
Pompey 22, 27, 32, 34
Populares 17–18
Ptolemy XIII 32
Remus 9
Rhea Silva 9
Rhodes 5
Romulus 9
Rubicon River 27
Senate 16, 34
slaves 5, 8, 11, 16, 25
Sulla 18, 22
Tiber River 9
Transalpine Gaul 22
Triumvirate 22, 27